NATURAL WONDERS OF THE WORLD

THE SAHARA DESERT

by Rebecca Kraft Rector

FOCUS
READERS

WWW.FOCUSREADERS.COM

Focus Readers is distributed by North Star Editions:
sales@northstareditions.com | 888-417-0195

Produced for Focus Readers by Red Line Editorial.

Content Consultant: Jeffrey R. Walker, PhD, Professor of Earth Science, Vassar College

Photographs ©: hadynyah/iStockphoto, cover, 1; yakthai/Shutterstock Images, 4–5; Saida Shigapova/Shutterstock Images, 7, 10–11, 22–23; sunsinger/Shutterstock Images, 9; Red Line Editorial, 13, 19; Dmitry Pichugin/Shutterstock Images, 15; Mikadun/Shutterstock Images, 16–17; Cat Downie/Shutterstock Images, 21; Quick Shot/Shutterstock Images, 24–25; Ready-made/Shutterstock Images, 27; tupatu76/Shutterstock Images, 29

ISBN
978-1-63517-517-2 (hardcover)
978-1-63517-589-9 (paperback)
978-1-63517-733-6 (ebook pdf)
978-1-63517-661-2 (hosted ebook)

Library of Congress Control Number: 2017948098

Printed in the United States of America
Mankato, MN
November, 2017

ABOUT THE AUTHOR

Rebecca Kraft Rector is a writer, librarian, and researcher. She is the author of novels, nonfiction books, and more than 100 nonfiction articles.

TABLE OF CONTENTS

CHAPTER 1

HOT AND DRY

The sun beats down on the desert sands. The temperature rises. A hot wind blows the sand into a whirlwind. Small animals hide in tunnels under the sand. Others find shelter among the rocks. Such is life in the Sahara Desert, the largest hot desert in the world.

The Sahara is the world's third-largest desert, behind Antarctica and the Arctic Desert.

A desert is a very dry area that gets little rain. The Sahara includes parts of at least 11 countries or territories in North Africa. The desert covers 3.5 million square miles (9.1 million sq km). This is approximately the size of the United States. However, the size of the Sahara changes over time. It gets bigger and smaller.

Sand **dunes** in the Sahara can reach as high as 500 feet (152 meters). But only one-fourth of the Sahara is sand. Most of the desert is rocky. There are plains, plateaus, and some mountains. Wadis are dry streambeds. If rain falls, the wadis fill with water.

Trees grow at an oasis in the Sahara in Morocco.

Desert plants and animals have **adapted** to the difficult conditions in the Sahara. Plants, animals, and people are often found near an **oasis**. An oasis is a place with underground water.

The Atlas Mountains are in the north of the Sahara. The desert also contains other mountain ranges. These include the Tibesti and the Ahaggar.

Two permanent rivers are near the edges of the Sahara. These are the Nile in the east and the Niger in the southwest. The Sahara also has approximately 20 lakes. However, only Lake Chad has water that is drinkable. The other lakes have salt water.

EXTREME WEATHER

On a summer day, the Sahara is the hottest region in the world. Temperatures often reach above 120 degrees Fahrenheit (49°C). However, the temperature drops significantly at night. It becomes cold and may even freeze in the winter. Rain is rare in the Sahara. Snow sometimes falls in the mountains. Hot, dry winds are common. They sometimes create sandstorms.

A nomad moves through the Sahara in Algeria.

People live in the Sahara. Most settle near an oasis. However, some travel around the desert with their animals. They do not live in one place. They are called nomads.

CHAPTER 2

FORMING THE SAHARA

The Sahara as we know it is relatively new. Tiny changes in the tilt of Earth's **axis** cause the area to change over time. The Sahara has gone through periods of being wet and green. Grasslands grew, and lakes were filled with water. But over tens of thousands of years, the land dried into the desert that exists now.

The Sahara has existed in some form for thousands of years.

The present-day Sahara probably changed from wet to dry approximately 5,000 years ago.

Scientists disagree on how the Sahara originally formed. They also disagree on how old the Sahara is. One theory says the desert formed two to three million years ago. This would have been at the beginning of the most recent ice age, which occurred between 2.5 million and 11,000 years ago. During an ice age, there is less rain and water at lower latitudes. As a result, the Sahara became very dry.

A new theory suggests the Sahara might be much older. The theory is based on the fact that Earth's surface is made up of huge plates. These plates move very slowly across a layer of melted rock. When these plates collide, they can create earthquakes and volcanoes. They can also create mountains.

MAP OF THE SAHARA DESERT

MOROCCO

TUNISIA

N
W   E
S

WESTERN SAHARA

ALGERIA

LIBYA

EGYPT

MAURITANIA

MALI

NIGER

CHAD

SUDAN

ERITREA

SENEGAL

BURKINA FASO

AFRICA

■ Sahara Desert

Seven million years ago, the Alps and the Himalayan mountain ranges were created. They closed off a large sea. The sea grew smaller and smaller. Part of the sea was replaced by land. This land blocked winds that carried rain into the Sahara. As a result, the desert formed.

DINOSAURS OF THE SAHARA

The Sahara is so dry that **fossils** are well preserved there. Many dinosaur fossils have been discovered. Millions of years ago, the Sahara was not a desert. The largest meat-eating dinosaur lived in this region. Known as Spinosaurus, the dinosaur swam in rivers. Fossils of other dinosaurs have also been found. Pterosaurs and a **species** of enormous crocodiles lived in the Sahara, too.

Sandstone cliffs formed over many years in Algeria.

Studies of rocks support the idea that the Sahara first formed two to three million years ago. However, computer models and studies of ancient sand dunes suggest that the Sahara formed closer to seven million years ago.

CHAPTER 3

A HOSTILE HOME

The plants and animals in the Sahara live in high temperatures and with little water. The water in the oases supports many of the species. Other species live in the Atlas Mountains and on the coast. There is more rain and water in those areas.

Hostile conditions make life challenging in much of the Sahara.

More than 1,600 plant species live in the Sahara. Plants such as grasses and thyme might grow in the driest areas, but very little else grows there. Many of the plants that do live there have developed long roots to reach the underground water. On certain plants, roots are as long as 80 feet (24 m). Some dry desert plants flower and produce seeds quickly when it rains. But the seeds must wait for the next rain in order to grow.

Oases and mountains have more water for plants to grow. Typical oasis plants include shrubs, grasses, and palm trees. In the highlands, olive trees, cypress, and acacias can be found.

DEEP ROOTS

The acacia tree is one of the few plants that can survive in the Sahara. Its root system has adapted to survive there. Some roots go deep underground to find water. Others stay near the surface to capture rainwater.

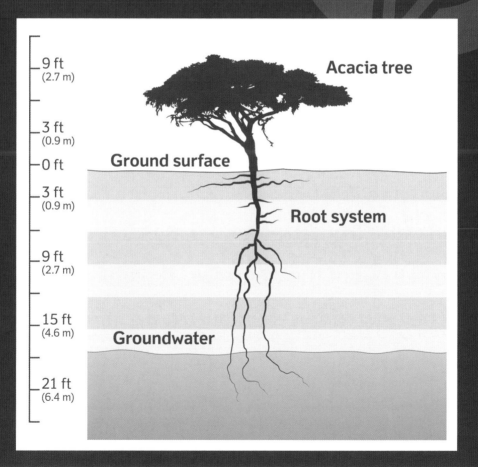

9 ft (2.7 m)

3 ft (0.9 m)

0 ft

3 ft (0.9 m)

9 ft (2.7 m)

15 ft (4.6 m)

21 ft (6.4 m)

Acacia tree

Ground surface

Root system

Groundwater

Animals in the Sahara have adapted so they can stay cool and use less water. Some animals stay underground during the day, when temperatures are hottest. They come out at night to find food. The fennec fox and the jerboa, a small rodent, are two examples of this kind of animal. They also have other adaptations. The fennec fox has very large ears. These ears help release heat. The jerboa only takes in water from the food it eats. Scorpions come out of their burrows at night, too. They also get water only from their food.

Frogs, toads, and crocodiles live in lakes and oases. Crocodiles hide in caves and burrows if the water dries up. They

Adaptations help animals such as the fennec fox survive with little access to water.

come out when it rains again. Deadly snakes and other animals live in the sand.

There are more than 300 bird species in the Sahara. Ostriches can run nearly 40 miles per hour (64 km/h). This helps them outrun predators. Other birds include owls, eagles, and waterbirds.

THE CAMEL

Humans have used camels in the Sahara since at least 2000 BCE. Camels can carry goods and people. Their meat and milk have helped desert people survive. A camel's hair can also be made into clothes and tents.

Camels are well adapted to desert life. Most camels in the Sahara have one hump. They store fat in their humps. The fat can be used for energy when they cannot find food. Their stomachs can hold 25 gallons (95 L) of water. This allows them to go for two or more weeks without water.

Other adaptations help, too. Thick eyelashes protect their eyes from sand. Their nostrils can close against blowing sand. Wide, soft pads on their feet also make it easier to walk in the sand.

Camels help many people survive in the Sahara Desert's harsh conditions.

CHAPTER 4

THE SAHARA DESERT TODAY

Conditions in the Sahara make it difficult for humans to survive there. However, people have long called the Sahara home. Native tribes still live there today. The Tuareg people are mostly nomads. They herd goats and sheep. The Moors are farmers of date palms.

A Tuareg boy rests with his camel.

Tourists also visit the Sahara. They stay mostly on the edges of the desert. Four-wheel-drive vehicles are often used to travel in the desert. Some travelers prefer to ride camels. If tourists go into

SURVIVING IN THE SAHARA

People, animals, and plants need water to survive. Many people live in the oases because water can be found there. They grow crops and raise animals. Nomads stay on the move. They search the desert for grass for their animals to eat. They live in tents. When the grass is gone, they move. Nomads wear **turbans** and long robes as protection against the sun and sand. They eat dates from palms in the oases. Goat and camel milk is made into cheese.

Tourists explore the Sahara on camels.

the desert, they leave the towns behind. They must sleep in tents or in the open.

The Sahara is a unique place. But climate change threatens to change it forever. Higher temperatures disturb the balance of nature. **Habitats** may become drier. Water holes could dry up. If plants die, animals might seek new homes.

Human activities are also a threat to the Sahara. Resources such as iron, copper, and manganese are found in the Sahara. Oil and natural gas are also present. Digging for these resources harms the environment. And the chemicals that workers use can poison animals. Another threat occurs when people allow their animals to eat too many plants in one area. When this happens, the plants in that location may not be able to grow back. Off-road vehicles can destroy habitats as well.

Human activities are also helping to protect the Sahara. Protected areas and national parks limit human activity. Areas

The sand cracks in a dried-up lake in the Sahara.

have also been chosen as World Heritage sites. This means they have value to the entire world. Efforts like these could help protect the Sahara for years to come.

FOCUS ON
THE SAHARA DESERT

Write your answers on a separate piece of paper.

1. Write a letter to a friend describing how the Sahara formed.

2. Would you like to ride a camel in the Sahara? Why or why not?

3. Which animal has very large ears that help release heat?

> **A.** fennec fox
> **B.** jerboa
> **C.** crocodile

4. What might happen if animals did not adapt to the desert?

> **A.** Animals would drink up all the water.
> **B.** Animals would die from the harsh conditions.
> **C.** Animals would stay cool.

Answer key on page 32.

GLOSSARY

adapted
To have changed to better function in a certain place or situation.

axis
An imaginary line from the North Pole to the South Pole that the planet Earth spins around.

dunes
Hills of sand.

fossils
Parts of an animal or plant that remain preserved in rock.

habitats
The type of places where plants or animals normally grow or live.

oasis
A place in the desert where there are plants and water.

species
A group of animals or plants that are similar.

tourists
People who visit an area for recreation.

turbans
Head coverings made of long pieces of cloth wrapped around the head.

TO LEARN MORE

BOOKS

Aloian, Molly. *The Sahara Desert*. New York: Crabtree Publishing, 2013.

Hinman, Bonnie. *Keystone Species That Live in Deserts*. Hockessin, DE: Mitchell Lane Publishers, 2016.

Miller, Mirella S. *Desert Ecosystems*. Mankato, MN: 12-Story Library, 2018.

NOTE TO EDUCATORS

Visit **www.focusreaders.com** to find lesson plans, activities, links, and other resources related to this title.

INDEX

Answer Key: 1. Answers will vary; **2.** Answers will vary; **3.** A; **4.** B